D1629588

CHILDREN'S BOOK
of
WILD FLOWERS

BY

NANCY MILLER

IN FOUR PARTS WITH 64 PLATES
IN FULL COLOUR

W. & R. CHAMBERS LTD.
EDINBURGH AND LONDON

List of Colour Plates

First Published 1952

Printed in Great Britain by T. & A. Constable, Ltd., Edinburgh

WOOD ANEMONE

LOOKING AT FLOWERS

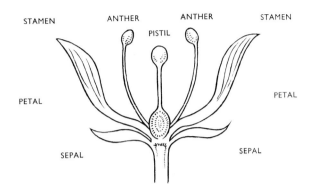

LOOKING at flowers is much more interesting when we know each one by name. Some flowers are easily recognised by colour and shape, others by scent, or even by leaves. There are, however, certain parts of the flower at which we should look carefully, and which have special names.

When the flower is still in bud, it is very delicate, and must have a protection against cold winds. Nearly every bud has a warm covering folded closely round it. Sometimes the covering is in one piece, like a cup. More often it is made up of five or six or more pieces, and these separate pieces are called *Sepals*. The sepals are usually green.

Most easily seen when you look at an open flower are usually the *Petals*. These are what the sepals have been guarding till it is time for them to unfold. It is of the petals that we speak most often when we describe a flower. We are not the only ones to be attracted by their soft silkiness.

The petals play a very special part in the life of the plant. They attract to the flower the bees and other insects which carry life from one plant to another.

If you look into the centre of the flower, you will see the *Stamens*. Without these, there could be no new seeds from which to grow new flowers. The stamens are usually slender threads growing either singly or in groups at the heart of the flower. Each stamen has a fat little head, called an *Anther*, filled with yellow powder called *Pollen*. It is the pollen which the insects carry from one flower to another, and which is needed to make the new seeds grow. The pollen is brought to the *Pistil*, which can be seen in the very centre of the ring of stamens.

Once the petals have done their work, and the insects have safely carried the pollen to and fro, the flower-heads fade. But it is wrong to say that the plant is dying. It is more alive than ever. The tiny seeds have begun to ripen in readiness for their part in the story, and the life of the plant never stops.

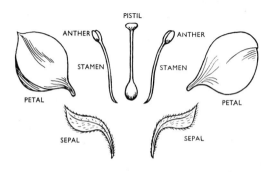

5

WOODY NIGHTSHADE   HONEYSUCKLE

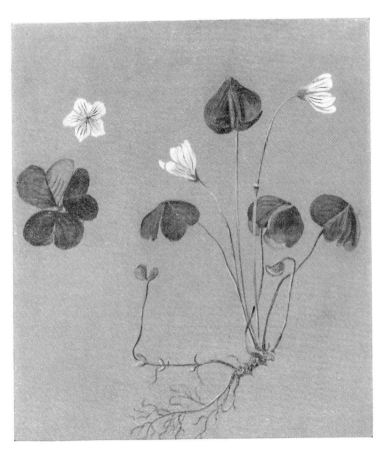

WOOD SORREL

WOOD ANEMONE

Perhaps you will know this flower better by its other name, Windflower. If you watch it when the wind is blowing, you will see the flower sway on its stalk, and turn its back to the wind, like a weather-cock.

Because it blooms so early, about the time when the first cuckoo is heard, the Wood Anemone is sometimes called Cuckoo Flower. This is a common name for flowers which appear in very early Spring.

The Wood Anemone is one of the flowers which have no petals. The six sepals are large and white. On the outside they are often tinged purple or pink. The buds of the Anemone look pink until they open. Within the sepals are the yellow heads of the stamens, and in the centre of them again is a green knot of seeds. The leaves are each divided into three, very deeply cut into round the edges, and their short stalks are covered with fine hairs. If you find a Wood Anemone root, you will probably think it is a tough brown piece of stick.

WOODY NIGHTSHADE

This plant attracts attention by its flowers. The five petals are purple, with green spots near the centre. Sticking out from their midst is a bright-yellow cone. You can see these flowers first of all in June, and they bloom through the Summer.

The leaves are broad and pointed, and the upper ones have little leaflets beside them, like pairs of ears.

When the flowers have gone, you will still see the Woody Nightshade in the hedges, because of its clusters of bright-red berries. These are not at all good to eat, and should be left severely alone. They hold the seeds which in time may grow into new plants.

HONEYSUCKLE

THE sweet-scented Honeysuckle is another plant which twines itself round the hedge-stems. Because of this, its other name is Wood-bine, or Wood-bind.

The trumpet-shaped flowers appear in June, and go on until September or October. Usually they are a mixture of yellow, pink and red. The heads of the stamens, and the long green tip of the seed-vessel, stick out from the mouth of each trumpet. Of all the flowers, the Honeysuckle is the most loved by insects for the sweetness at its centre. When the bees cannot reach this, other insects do so, by making little holes at the foot of the flower-tube.

Later on, the seeds grow into deep-red berries, of which the birds are very fond.

The leaves of the Honeysuckle are very smooth, and are covered all over with tiny veins.

BLUEBELL OR WILD HYACINTH

BINDWEED

WOOD SORREL

THIS is one of the most delicate of all Spring flowers. If the day is dark or cold, even the leaves will fold up. These leaves are heart-shaped, and rather like those of the Clover. They rise on slender pink stalks, and are green on top, with purple shading underneath. They are divided into three leaflets, each with a deep fold down the centre. People once used them in salads, but they taste sour.

The five petals of the Wood Sorrel make a white bell, veined with lilac. They hang from the green cup formed by the five pointed sepals. The seeds grow up in a case, which splits when touched, and throws them quite a distance from the parent plant.

The Wood Sorrel was once thought to be useful for curing cuts and wounds.

A Welsh name for this plant is Fairy Bells, from the shape of the flower-heads.

Some people think that the Wood Sorrel, and not the three-leaved Clover, is the true Shamrock of Ireland.

WILD HYACINTH

ENGLISH children know this Spring flower as the Bluebell. It grows from a bulb, deeply buried in the ground. The bulb acts as a store-house for the food which is needed by the growing plant. Above ground, the leaves appear first. They are long and narrow, and look as though someone had folded them in the middle and forgotten to flatten them out again.

The pale-blue flowers grow on one side of a long juicy stalk. Each flower forms a drooping bell, and has a short stalk of its own. The bells are divided into six parts, which curl back. So many of them cluster together that the flower has been given the name Ring o' Bells.

You will always find Wild Hyacinths growing closely together.

BINDWEED

This is another plant which gets its name from its habit of binding itself to the hedges. Even its stem is twisted like a piece of rope. The leaves are smooth, and shaped like hearts. The white bell-shaped flowers grow on stalks of their own, just beside the leaves. The edges of the bell are waved. The flower is held secure by two heart-shaped leaflets.

The white blossoms open to their fullest extent in bright sunshine, and close again at the threat of rain. They last for only a day, but so many buds are ready to take their places that such swift fading is hardly noticed.

Notice how wonderfully the flower of the Bindweed is folded, when it is still in bud.

Look for the Bindweed during the Summer.

WILD STRAWBERRY

WOOD LOOSESTRIFE OR YELLOW PIMPERNEL

WILD STRAWBERRY

PROBABLY you do not think of this as a flower at all, because you prefer the fruit which appears after the flower has gone. But in the early Summer you will find the Wild Strawberry as a flower with five small white petals. Later on, when the petals have faded, the seed-vessel becomes a bright-red fruit, with little straw-coloured seeds clinging all over it. The leaves of the Wild Strawberry are dark-green and crinkled, with jagged edges.

The whole plant grows from a woody root. It sends out long green shoots which lie on the surface of the ground. These runners put out roots in their turn, and in time a new plant grows where they have taken hold of the soil.

WOOD LOOSESTRIFE

THE delicate Wood Loosestrife likes to grow in a shady place. Its weak trailing stem lies close to the ground, with little rootlets growing downwards. The glossy leaves grow in pairs, and where they join the stems the flower-stalks curve gracefully outwards.

The flowers are yellow and star-shaped, with five broad, pointed petals. They are very like those of another plant called the Scarlet Pimpernel, and because of that the Wood Loosestrife is sometimes known as the Yellow Pimpernel. A simpler name is Star-flower, from the shape made by the petals.

WILD ARUM

You will easily recognise the Wild Arum. Its leaves appear in early Spring, and look like long dark-green arrow-heads, covered with purplish-brown spots. In April or May there appears also a large pale-green sheath, folded round the stalk at its lower end, and opening out into a pointed hood. Sheltered by this is a little spike which stands up very straight and stiff. This spike may be pink or purple, but sometimes it is yellow.

 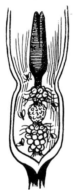 

Where are the flowers of the Arum? They are safe inside the spike, waiting for pollen to be brought to them from another Arum. This is done by tiny insects, which are attracted to the Arum spike. They force their way down into it, past the hairs which grow inside. Once in, they find themselves prisoners. As they try to force the hairs upwards, they lose the pollen they have brought, and get a fresh supply. The tiny hairs wither, and the insect flies away to another Arum.

WILD ARUM

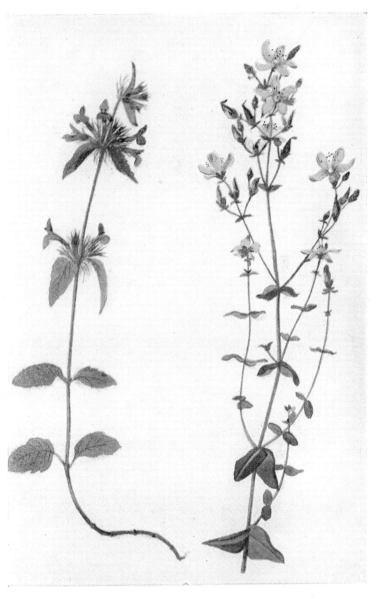

BASIL   ST. JOHN'S WORT

Later, the spike and its hood droop away, and there is left a mass of berries, green at first, then yellow, and lastly red. These hold the seeds of the Arum. They are pecked by birds and scattered over the ground. The berries are very pretty, but you should leave them for the birds. They can eat them quite safely, but they are harmful to us. The Arum has many attractive names, such as Monk's Hood and Lords and Ladies, but another of its names is the Poison Berry.

BASIL

You will probably be attracted to the Basil by its scent. The plant straggles over the hedges in late Summer and early Autumn. The leaves and stem are covered with little hairs, and are soft to the touch. The flowers are purple, or reddish-purple. They look like tubes which have been opened at the top into separate parts. They grow very close together, on short stalks round the stem just where the leaves appear. Beside the rings of flowers are many long, hairy bristles.

The Basil was given its odd name because it was once supposed to be a protection against a dreadful animal called a Basilisk. This animal was so frightening that no one dared to look at it, still less to fight against it. It was found, however, that anyone who armed himself with this flower was quite safe. The basilisk disliked it so much that it ran away at once.

ST JOHN'S WORT

Do not look for this flower until nearly the end of June. It was given its name because people noticed that it blossomed about the 24th of June, St John's Day.

There are many varieties of this plant, but the one shown in the picture is the Slender St John's Wort. It has a round smooth stem, with little branches growing outwards. On each branch are orange-tipped buds. When these open out, the starry flowers are deep-yellow. The stamens grow in the centre like a bush, and have deep-orange-coloured tips. The leaves have no stalks, and are rounded. Hold one of them up to the light, and you will see a great many little whitish dots, almost as though someone had pricked the leaf all over with a needle.

BROAD-LEAVED GARLIC

IF you are playing in the woods in Spring-time, and suddenly smell onions, you may be sure that the Broad-leaved Garlic is growing somewhere near. Its leaves are long and pointed, like spear heads. The flowers grow in white clusters at the top of long stems. Each is like a six-pointed star, in the centre of which are three green balls joined together. These hold the seeds of the future garlic plants.

BROAD-LEAVED GARLIC

PRIMROSE

The Broad-leaved Garlic is very pretty to look at, but because of its smell you would be wise to leave it where it is!

In the West of England, this plant is sometimes known by the unusual name of Moly. This was the name of a herb which was very highly thought of long ago, in Greece. It was supposed to be a certain guard against evil spells. Perhaps it was thought in England that the Broad-leaved Garlic was related to this wonderful herb.

PRIMROSE

In Spring no wood or hedge-bank is complete without its primroses. Because this flower is one of the signs of early Spring, it has been given its name, which means "first rose." It is not altogether right as a name, for the plant is neither the first of Spring, nor is it a rose! Long ago, however, the name rose was used for flowers not at all like our roses nowadays.

If the Primrose gets the moisture which it likes, the flower-stalks can grow quite long. Each stalk has one flower. A long tube is held in the narrow sepal-cup, and the mouth of the tube opens out into five pale-yellow sections. You may think the flower has five petals, but if you look carefully you will see that the sections are joined into one.

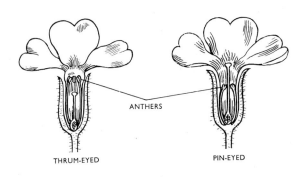

THRUM-EYED   ANTHERS   PIN-EYED

There are two kinds of Primrose flowers. In one, the stamens are gathered together at the top of the tube. This is the *thrum-eyed* primrose. In the other, the stamens are hidden, and what you see is a little green ball, like a pin-head, on the end of the slender stalk which rises from the seed-vessel. This is the *pin-eyed* primrose.

The Primrose leaves grow in a rosette, and have short juicy stalks. They are very crinkled and veined. The flowers come up from the centre of the rosette.

TRAVELLER'S JOY

THIS is another flower which has no petals. Instead it has four greenish-white sepals, and within them, many stamens of the same colour. In Summer, Traveller's Joy climbs right over the tops of the hedges. It can do this because of its leaf-stalks, which look frail and yet twine themselves strongly round the hedge-stems.

CLEMATIS OR TRAVELLER'S JOY

RED CAMPION

The leaves of the Clematis, as this plant is often called, are dark-green above and pale-green below. Their edges are sometimes smooth, and sometimes cut into like the teeth of a big saw.

If you look for Traveller's Joy in Autumn, you will see why it has been given its other name of Old Man's Beard. When the seeds begin to grow, they send out long white feathery tufts which wave on the hedges. They are carried away by passing animals, and the seeds are carried off too, to grow into new plants elsewhere.

RED CAMPION

THIS is a Summer flower, but it may be seen much earlier. You are most likely to find it in a damp place by a hedge. It can be quite a tall plant, with long, pointed leaves which grow in pairs. The stem is often red, and covered with fine hairs. If you crush both it and the leaves, they will give out a strong scent which you will not like very much.

The flower of the Red Campion has five reddish-pink petals, each almost cut into two. They look as though they are spilling out of the reddish-green cup of the sepals. Later on this cup acts as a covering for the seeds as they ripen. Unfortunately there is a moth which likes to lay its eggs at the foot of the cup. When the grub is hatched, it bores its way in and feeds on the Campion seeds. Then it lives safe and sheltered within the covering meant to protect the seeds.

The very centre of the flower looks like a small eye, or like a ring of very tiny white teeth. Because of this, the plant is sometimes known as Bird's Eye, or Robin's Eye. In some places, the Red Campion is known simply as Robin-flower.

WOOD SAGE

IT was once thought that this plant could make people wise. It was also looked upon as having great powers of healing.

It is in flower from July until August, and its other name is Wood Germander. It is the leaves which have the bitter taste which we know as sage. When crushed, they give off a strong smell. They are soft and wrinkled, and cut into teeth at the edges. Sometimes they are yellowish-green in colour.

The stem is square, and slightly branching. It is tough and woody at its foot, and tinged with red.

The pale-yellow flowers grow in branching spikes. Each has a long lower "lip" which hangs downwards. The purple stamens stick up so that their pollen can easily be transferred to any visiting insect.

One name for this plant is Hind-heal. This dates from the time when deer could still be hunted in the great forests which grew all over England. It was thought that when the hinds, the female deer, were hurt, they ate this plant and were cured.

WOOD SAGE

FOXGLOVE

FOXGLOVE

How many names do you know for the Foxglove?
Almost certainly most of them are connected with
fairies!

Into late Summer the Foxglove bells hang on
their stiff stems. They are usually purple or rose-
pink, but sometimes this can fade to white. Look
inside the bells and you will see many dark-purple
spots, surrounded by rings of white. The Foxglove
has a clever way of guarding its pollen. A network
of fine hairs keeps away all insects except those
which are the right size to carry off the pollen to
other foxgloves. When the petals fade, green cases
are left behind, crammed with seeds.

Remember to look at the lacy patterns on the
foxglove leaves. Sometimes these repeat the pink
shade of the bells.

WOOD BETONY

THIS plant is related to the Nettle, but it will not
sting you.

It is tall and square-stemmed. The edges of
the narrow, pointed leaves are cut into rounded
teeth. There is quite a distance between each
pair of leaves. The flowers bloom purple in late
June, and grow so closely that they make a spike.
This spike has no point, but is blunt at the top, as
though a piece had been cut off.

Long ago, Wood Betony was supposed to cure almost anything, even bad dreams. Because of this, the Welsh people thought of it in connection with one of their favourite saints, St Bride. One of the old Welsh names for the plant is St Bride's Comb.

Wood Betony was thought to be a sure charm against evil spirits, and as such was often worn round the neck. It was looked upon as one of the most precious of herbs.

WOOD BETONY

Children's Book of Wild Flowers

PART II.

List of Colour Plates

CORN MARIGOLD

DAISIES AND DANDELIONS
(Ray and Tube Florets)

IF you had to describe a Daisy, how would you do it? A ring of white petals round a yellow centre of stamens? That is what it looks like, but in fact the blossom of the Daisy is not one flower but many, and the "petals" are themselves tiny flowers. Together they make what is called a *composite* flower.

The little flowers are known as *florets*, and are of two kinds, tube florets and ray florets. In the Daisy the yellow centre is made up of many tube-shaped florets, and the white ring consists of strap-shaped ones, sticking out like rays. There may be as many as two hundred and fifty florets on one flower-head. At night, or if it is dull, the ray florets close and the flower shuts itself up.

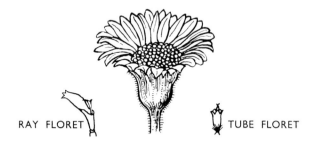

RAY FLORET   TUBE FLORET

The tube florets always open in strict order, the outer ones first, and so on inwards row by row. Insects are attracted to the Daisy by the contrasting colours of its white and yellow florets.

4

The Dandelion is another composite flower. It attracts insects by its brilliant yellow colour. The flower-head of the Dandelion is made up entirely of ray florets. They are much larger than those of the Daisy. When the bloom has withered, there is left the dandelion "clock," which is Nature's way of making sure that the seeds will be scattered. Each seed is attached by a long stalk to a little parachute of down. With the help of this it can float a long distance.

Many composite flowers distribute their seeds in this way. See how many are described in this book, and see how many you can find for yourself.

DANDELION CLOCK

DANDELION SEED

YARROW OR MILFOIL

WILD BEAKED PARSLEY OR COW CHERVIL

CORN MARIGOLD

THIS is like a big yellow daisy. The flower-head is made up of many complete florets. There is a button-like centre of tube florets, and a circle of ray florets sticks out all round. These are all yellow.

The Marigold is seen at its best amid ripening corn, but farmers do not admire it, as it harms the crops. It is a smooth plant, with a branching stem and jagged leaves. The upper leaves have no stalks, and clasp the main stem.

There are many names for the Corn Marigold. One of them is Moon-flower, because the golden circle reminds us of the full moon. Another name is Harvest-flower, although in fact the flowers may be seen at any time between June and October, or even later.

YARROW

YOU will know the Yarrow because of its feathery leaves. Each one is dark-green and divided into the many parts that have given the plant its second name of Milfoil, which means "thousand leaves."

The flowers grow in clusters at the end of stalks coming from the main stem. Several flower-heads grow on each stalk. They look like small daisies, but each "daisy" is made up of many small florets crowded together. The flower-heads have a dull-yellow centre, surrounded by a white frill.

The stem is stronger-looking than the rest of the plant, and is stiff. It is slightly tinged with red.

Yarrow is to be found in almost every meadow in Summer-time. It was once used a great deal in the healing of wounds. A very old name for the plant is Soldier's Wound-wort.

WILD BEAKED PARSLEY

This is one of a number of plants which have their flower-heads growing on stalks arranged like the ribs of an umbrella. It is one of the earliest, and when the flowers are in bud the umbrella-heads droop. Each of the tiny white flowers has five petals and five white-topped stamens. As often happens with these "umbrella" flowers, there are no sepals. Behind each cluster of flowers are five small leaflets which fold back towards the main stem. The stem itself is stiff and hollow. The lower part is covered with short hairs. The leaves are soft, and deeply fringed like those of a fern.

The plant may be easily recognised after its flowers have faded. Its seed-vessels ripen into green beak-like shapes, and that is why it is called Wild *Beaked* Parsley.

BIRD'S FOOT TREFOIL   WILD PANSY OR HEARTSEASE

AGRiMONY   SELF-HEAL

BIRD'S FOOT TREFOIL

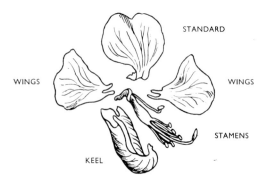

THIS is a Summer flower which grows nearly every-where. You will see its stems lying along the ground, for they are usually too weak to stand by themselves. The name "Trefoil" means "three leaves," but in fact this plant has five smooth leaflets growing on each stalk. There is a single one at the top, then a pair, and lastly another pair where the leaf-stalk joins the main stem.

The orange-yellow clusters of the flowers are easily seen. Each one has five petals. The top-most, called the standard, encloses the others when still in bud. The side petals are called the wings, and they partly enfold the two lowest petals which are joined together. These two are called the keel, because they look like that part of a ship. If you pull off the keel, you will find the seed-pod forming inside. The pods are long, hard, and shiny. When several are growing together, in different directions, they look like the claws of a bird. That is why this plant has been called Bird's Foot Trefoil.

There are many other names for the Trefoil. One of these is Shoes and Stockings, and another is Lady's Slipper. Can you think why the plant has been given these names?

WILD PANSY

All Summer the tiny faces of the Wild Pansies can be seen. The flowers have five petals, not all of the same colour. Two stand upright, and these are usually purple, while the others are yellow. The Wild Pansy is much smaller than the garden one. The five pointed green sepals do not fall when the petals do, but stay to hold the seed-vessel. When it is ripe, this splits to show three boat-shaped cases, each with its row of seeds.

The wavy-edged leaves grow on short stalks, and where they and the flower-stalks join the main stem there are other differently shaped leaflets. They are like little straps standing out round the stem.

The Wild Pansy was given its other name of Heartsease because it was thought that it could help people who were unhappy.

The word "Pansy" is simply another way of saying a French word which means "a thought."

GREATER PLANTAIN

DEVIL'S-BIT SCABIOUS

AGRIMONY

THE tall stem of the Agrimony is covered with short hairs, and on it the yellow flowers grow one above the other in tapering spikes. Those lowest down come out first, and show five widely-spreading petals. The sepal-cup is a green bell with five large points at its mouth.

After the petals fall, a green seed-vessel appears, fringed with hooked bristles. These cling to whatever they touch, and so the seeds are carried away, to grow into new Agrimony plants elsewhere.

The leaves are deeply cut round the edges, and grow in pairs, with one large leaf at the top of the stalk.

This plant was a favourite long ago, because it was thought to be very good as a medicine. The dried leaves can be used as a kind of tea.

The whole plant gives a yellow dye. The later in the year it is gathered, the darker the dye.

SELF-HEAL

FROM its name you will have guessed that the Self-heal was once supposed to heal cuts. It was thought of as being specially useful to carpenters and farmers. From this, it was called Herb Carpenter. Farmers made use of it when they cut themselves with their sickles, and so yet another name for the plant was Sickle-wort.

It begins by creeping along the ground, and then sends up several grooved stems. The narrow heart-shaped leaves are rough, and sometimes outlined in brown.

The flowers grow close together in rings, one above the other. Beneath each ring are two pointed leaflets. Each flower stands in a flattened reddish-brown tube. The flower itself is like a gaping mouth, and the upper lip is curved like a sickle. The bluish-purple of the Self-heal can be seen throughout the Summer.

GREATER PLANTAIN

You may not think of this as a flower at all. Its other name of Mouse-tail well describes the appearance of the small colourless flowers which grow packed together in a long spike at the end of a stiff stalk. When the stamens appear, they have purple tips.

The leaves grow in a rosette, closely pressed to the ground. They are frilled at the edges and have a crumpled appearance.

Birds are very fond of the seeds of the Greater Plantain.

In olden times the Plantain was supposed to cure all sorts of illnesses. People going on long journeys placed a leaf of it inside their shoes, because they believed that that would keep them from feeling tired, or from getting blisters on their feet.

COW PARSNIP OR HOGWEED

WHITE DEAD NETTLE   RED DEAD NETTLE

The Plantain is sometimes called Way-bread, which may be another way of saying way-*bred*, as it is usually to be found by the way-side.

Plantain seeds are carried very easily, even from one continent to another. The North American Indians called this plant by a name which meant " White Man's foot," because it seemed to spring up wherever the white settlers made their appearance.

DEVIL'S-BIT SCABIOUS

THIS plant got its strange name because its root looks as though someone had bitten it off at the end. It was thought that the root had great healing powers, and this made the devil so angry that he bit it off!

It is a slender plant, and you will not see its bluish-purple flowers before July. The flower-heads are really clusters of very small flowers, and they look like balls cut in half.

The leaves are long and hairy, and rough to the touch. Sometimes the upper ones are cut at the edges.

COW PARSNIP

THIS is an umbrella flower which is easily recognised because it is so tall. The stiff hairy stems can grow as high as six feet. They are hollow, and in Winter they are used by insects which creep into them for shelter.

The leaves are hairy and deeply cut. The flowers begin their lives inside green knobs close to the stem. The bud grows until it bursts its covering and pushes out a stalk of its own. The flowers grow in flat masses at the end of stiff green spokes. In the centre of each cluster are green buds, and all round, a ring of tiny white flowers. When the flowers have withered, the spokes of the umbrella remain.

This plant is sometimes called Hogweed, because pigs are so fond of its leaves. They fatten upon them very quickly.

In some parts of Europe, the country people dry the stalks of the Cow Parsnip in the sun. From them they take a sugary substance which they eat as a sweet.

DEAD NETTLE (White and Red)

THESE are called "Dead" because, unlike the Stinging Nettle, they will do you no harm.

The White Dead Nettle grows taller than the Red, and its heart-shaped leaves are larger. The flowers grow in rings just above each pair of leaves. The petals are joined in a tube which divides at the mouth. The upper part stands up like a hood, and the lower makes a platform for the insects which come in search of the sweetness in the flower-tubes. Four black stamens can easily be seen sticking out from each tube.

DWARF RED RATTLE   YELLOW RATTLE

FUMITORY

The Red Dead Nettle is a more spreading plant. The stem is weak and hollow. The small purplish-red flowers crowd together amongst the upper leaves. They are shaped in the same way as those of the White Dead Nettle. The leaves may be of different shapes, but they always have scalloped edges. They often take on the purplish-red colour which gives the plant its name.

RED AND YELLOW RATTLE

THE Red Rattle lies close to the ground. Its leaves are deeply cut into at the edges. The bright-pink flowers grow from a puffy green-and-brown sepal-cup. Each flower has a long tube which becomes wider at the mouth and breaks into two. The upper part bends over like a hood and shelters the stamens. The lower part folds back. After the petals fall, the sepal-cup swells into a small bladder, and on a windy day the seeds can be heard rattling inside it.

The Yellow Rattle is more erect. The flowers are yellow and do not have the long tube of the Red Rattle. The seed-bladders are larger and flatter, and because of this some people call the plant Penny Rattle. The leaves have no stalks, and are long and deeply veined. Among the flowers are some leaves which are shorter and broader than the others.

FUMITORY

THERE are two kinds of Fumitory—Common and Ramping. Ramping Fumitory is long and straggling, and twines itself round other plants.

Common Fumitory grows more upright. Its flowers are in loose clusters. Those lowest down the stem come out first. They are rose-pink, but are often purple-tipped, especially before they are fully out. The four petals are joined in a tube which is curved at the end. The stamens and seed-vessel are hidden inside this tube. A small piece of one petal is not joined to the others, but hangs by itself like a pink tongue. This will help you to recognise the Fumitory.

Ramping Fumitory has yellow flowers. When the flowers fade, they change to chalky-grey. The feathery leaves are grey-green, and the delicate Fumitory looks like a wreath of smoke at the foot of the hedges.

COLT'S FOOT

THIS is a very early plant, and it is remarkable because the flowers appear *before* the leaves. They grow at the end of straight stalks which are covered with what look like pink scales. There are many tiny flowers so tightly massed together that they appear as one big yellow flower-head. When they have faded, in their place appears a fluffy ball of down which has attached to it the seeds of the new plants.

COLT'S FOOT

CONVOLVULUS OR FIELD BINDWEED   VIPER'S BUGLOSS

When the leaves do come, they can grow very big. They are often covered with a grey film which can be rubbed off. They are silvery underneath and green above. In shape they are roughly like the hoof of an animal, and so the plant is called Colt's Foot.

Because the Colt's Foot likes to grow in soil which has plenty of clay, it has been given the other name of Clay-weed.

It is yet another plant which was much used as a medicine. Long ago, if you had a bad cold or a cough, Colt's Foot might be used as part of the remedy for it.

CONVOLVULUS

THE very word Convolvulus suggests something twisting and twining. This plant is unwelcome in the fields because it winds itself round other plants, and is difficult to get rid of. It grows from a very small piece of root, and raises itself by means of its twisting stems.

The leaves are broad and pointed, like arrow-heads. The bell-shaped flowers are usually pink and white. They fit into small green cups. They can be seen as early as June, and as late as the Autumn.

Because it is so like the Greater Bindweed, this plant is sometimes called the Field or Lesser Bind-weed. Its flowers are about half the size of those on the Greater Bindweed.

VIPER'S BUGLOSS

You will know this plant by the brilliant blue of its bell-shaped flowers. These are pink in bud, but change colour later. Four stamens stand out from the petals and are easily seen by insects.

Behind each row of flowers is one of narrow, pointed leaves. These unfold along with the flower buds. The main leaves are rough and hairy, and they usually wither by the time the flowers appear. The stem is stiff, and it is covered with dark spots. Perhaps this is why the plant is connected with the viper, which has dark markings on its back. It was thought, too, that the plant contained a liquid which could cure snake-bite.

In its general appearance, Viper's Bugloss is so stiff and bristly that it is known in some places as Blue Thistle.

HERB ROBERT

This can be found at all times of the year, and its red stems and deeply cut, reddish leaves make it even more easily seen in Winter than in Summer. The whole plant is in different shades of red.

The flowers have five pinkish-red petals, and they grow in pairs at the end of short stalks. After the petals have fallen, a long spike appears in the midst of the sepals. This looks like the long pointed bill of a crane, and so the plant has been called Crane's Bill.

HERB ROBERT

SCARLET POPPY

The spike holds the new seeds. When these are ripe, green threads uncurl from its foot. At the end of each thread is a seed. Soon the threads break, and the seeds fall to the ground.

The name Herb Robert has many explanations. Some people think that "Robert" is the mischievous fairy Robin Goodfellow, or Puck as he is sometimes called. Others connect the plant with the outlaw Robin Hood. Still others think that it is named after St Robert, because the flower appears each year about the 24th of April, which is St Robert's Day.

The plant was once very highly thought of as a medicine. It was used to stop bleeding, and people said that this power was shown by the red colour of the leaves as they faded.

SCARLET POPPY

THIS is one of the most common of our wild flowers. The four bright-red petals make it easily seen, especially in the cornfields. When the bud has just opened, the petals are closely folded and crinkled, but after a little sunshine they become smooth and silky. Sometimes a purple spot can be seen at the foot of each petal.

In the centre of the flower is a green bowl, with a lid. This holds the Poppy seeds, and when they are ripe they pour out through little holes which open just below the lid. A ring of black-headed stamens stands round the seed-bowl.

The two hairy sepals fall off whenever the flower opens.

The leaves are long and jagged. The stems of the Wild Poppy are covered with bristles which stick straight out.

An insect called the Drapery Bee, or Poppy Bee, makes very clever use of the brightly-coloured petals of the Poppy. It cuts out the petals of a half-opened flower, strengthens the folds, and hangs these "curtains" over the walls of the cells in which it places its honey.

FIELD GENTIAN

This is a small, upright plant. Its purplish stems are crowded with leaves and flowers. The pointed leaves grow in pairs, and clasp the stem. They are quite plain round the edges.

The flowers are on purplish stalks, and have four lilac-blue petals joined together in a tube. At the mouth of the tube, the petals fold back, and a blue fringe can be seen. The flowers open only when the sun is shining very brightly. There are four blue-green sepals—two broad ones folded over two narrow, pointed ones.

You will have to look very carefully in order to see our Field Gentian against its background in the open fields where it likes to grow. Do not look for it too early in the Summer, for it does not bloom usually until August or even September.

FIELD GENTIAN   GROUNDSEL

GROUNDSEL

IF you have ever fed a pet canary, you will know how fond it is of the seeds of this plant. The flowers appear all the year round, and the flower-heads are made up of many small yellow tubes tightly packed together. These grow in a green cup made of narrow leaves pressed so closely that only the tips of the flowers can be seen.

When the flowers have withered, a bunch of white down takes their place. With the help of these tufts, the many brown seeds can float to the ground when they are ripe.

The Groundsel has a mass of roots, from which grows the soft, juicy stem.

The leaves are dark-green, and very jagged.

Children's Book of Wild Flowers

PART III.

List of Colour Plates

SCARLET PIMPERNEL

WHAT THE LEAVES DO

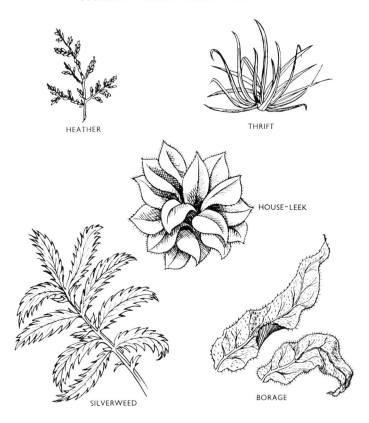

HEATHER

THRIFT

HOUSE-LEEK

SILVERWEED

BORAGE

If we leave a plant without water, it soon withers. It needs to keep on drawing in moisture to replace what it loses into the air. The leaves of a plant help it to keep this balance.

Many of the plants described in this book grow in waste-places, where there is little food or drink for them. Their leaves have different ways of making the most of their supplies.

4

Some plants, such as Heather, have many tiny leaves. This means that not too much moisture is lost through them.

Other leaves, like those of the Borage, are covered with hairs. This protects them and keeps the cold air from them.

When a plant likes to grow in a specially dry place, you will find that its leaves are thick and fleshy. Such a plant is the House-leek. It stores moisture in its leaves, and so does not need to draw it all the time from the soil.

In shape, the leaves are exactly suited to each particular plant and the place in which it grows. For example, a divided leaf allows more sunlight to reach the rest of the plant than a big, single leaf does. Narrow, grass-like leaves also let the light through to help the growth of the plant.

The leaves always grow out from the stem in an ordered arrangement. They may be on alternate sides, or they may grow in different sizes in such a way that one does not shade another. Some plants have their leaves growing in rosettes, close to the ground. This is a good way of making sure that sunlight reaches all of them equally.

However they grow, and in whatever shape, the leaves are very important to the life of the plant.

They are the plant's food factories. They breathe in gases from the air, and turn them into nourishment with the help of the sun's rays. The chief food they make is sugar, which the plant needs in order to grow.

CINQUEFOIL   TORMENTIL

LING OR HEATHER

SCARLET PIMPERNEL

WHEN it is dull, this flower closes up, and so it has been given the name of Poor Man's Weather-glass.

The flowers grow on four-sided stalks which are very easily broken. There are five red petals joined together to make a wheel. Between their edges you can see the points of the five narrow green sepals. The stamens in the centre have bright-yellow heads.

When the petals fall, a silvery-green ball is left, and this holds the seeds. Later on, the top half of the ball falls away and shows the seeds, which at a touch are sent flying away from the plant.

The pale-green leaves grow from the stems, without stalks. They are small and oval. Underneath, they are covered with little dark dots.

CINQUEFOIL

THIS is a French name meaning "five leaves." The leaves of the Cinquefoil grow in groups of five leaflets, spread out like the fingers and thumb of your hand. The edges are uneven, like the teeth of a saw. Both leaves and flowers have long slender stalks. The flowers have five yellow petals which show between them the green sepals. In the centre is a ring of yellow stamens.

The Cinquefoil is very difficult to get rid of. It grows from a small root like a carrot. From this, the stems go creeping away on the surface in all directions. In their turn, they send down little roots as they go, and these peg the plant firmly to the ground.

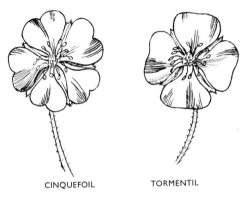

CINQUEFOIL   TORMENTIL

TORMENTIL

IT was once thought that this plant could cure toothache!

It looks a little like the Cinquefoil, but you will know it because it has only four yellow petals, and not five. Each petal is a complete heart-shape. The sepals behind make an eight-pointed green star. Each flower has its own stalk, growing from between a leaf and the stem. All the leaves are narrow and have edges cut into large teeth. Some have short stalks, while others come straight from the stem.

The root is woody to look at, but inside it is red in colour.

THRIFT   WILD THYME

BORAGE

LING

You have all seen Ling, or Heather, growing in purple masses on our moors and hills. Look carefully at the small bell-shaped blooms. They are unlike most flowers, for the petals are almost entirely hidden by the long sepals. These are the same colour as the petals, and they are dry and rustling, like tissue paper. Below the sepals are four green leaflets, which you may think at first are the sepals themselves.

The leaves are very tiny, and grow close together on shoots from the main branches. When they wither they turn a beautiful brownish-red.

The stems are wiry and tough. They are very springy, and twist in all directions. They can grow from one to three feet in height.

THRIFT

This plant can live upon very little. It likes a rocky cliff-top, where you may often see its cushions of grass-like leaves. The long flower-stalks rise from the centre of these. There is a downward-pointing sheath and then the pink flower-head. Each flower has five petals, and several flowers crowd together to make one head. When the blooms fade, the flower-head becomes brown and dry.

Perhaps you know the Thrift better by its other name of Sea Pink. It is so called because it looks rather like the Pinks which grow in the garden.

WILD THYME

You will always know when you are treading upon Wild Thyme, because of the perfume which you will be crushing out.

The plant trails along the ground in a tangle of stems and tiny leaves. It is a little tree, which creeps instead of growing upright. Some of the stems do grow upwards, and these carry the masses of small purple flowers.

The flowers crowd together in loose spikes. Each blossom is a purple tube set in a deep sepal-cup. The tube opens at the mouth and is cut in two. The upper half has a small notch in the centre, and the lower half is divided into three.

The plant likes to grow in dry places.

BORAGE

This is not a very common plant. It has a round hairy stem, and the dusty grey-green leaves are also covered with bristly hairs. The leaves have no stalks, and are of different shapes. Because of their roughness, one of the plant's older names was Ox-tongue.

You will know the Borage by its flowers. In bud they are reddish-purple, but later they are deep-blue. There are five pointed petals, and between them you can see the five green sepals, making a

REST-HARROW

SPEAR PLUME THISTLE

star shape. In the centre, the purple—almost black—stamens form a cone round the white seed-vessel. Little purple horns rise from the back of each stamen.

You will find the Borage in bloom during Summer and early Autumn.

One of the pleasant beliefs about this plant was that if you were feeling at all unhappy, it could make you glad again.

REST-HARROW

THIS plant was given its unusual name because of its root. It is so thick and tough that it is very difficult to tear up. It lies near the surface of the soil, and is strong enough to keep the harrow from being dragged smoothly over the ground.

The plant sometimes stands up like a small bush, but usually it is lower, with creeping stems. These are tough, and covered with soft hairs. The leaves, too, are hairy, and often egg-shaped. They can be quite sticky.

The flowers are pink and red. There are five petals, arranged in the same way as those of the Bird's Foot Trefoil. There is the standard on top, the two wings are at the side, and the keel is at the foot, hiding the stamens. The flowers have scarcely any stalks. They grow close to the main stem, and fit into green sepal-cups.

SPEAR PLUME THISTLE

This is a fearsome-looking plant, with all its sharp prickles. You will have to treat it with great care!

The leaves are set everywhere with strong spear-like points. Even the flowers grow out of a prickly ball which becomes larger as the flower-head opens. Each flower is made up of hundreds of purple florets. When these have gone, their place is taken by the feathery plumes of the thistledown. Each tuft has a tiny seed at one end, and floats it gently to the ground at a puff of wind.

It is said that this is the kind of Thistle which once saved a Scottish army. One dark night, a band of fierce Danes was about to attack the Scots. Suddenly, one of the Danes trod on the sharp prickles of a Thistle. The cry he gave roused the Scots and gave warning of the nearness of the enemy. The Danes were driven off, and the Thistle became the emblem of Scotland.

HOP CLOVER

You will know this by its flowers. They cluster in round yellow heads like tiny clovers. Each is made up of many florets closely packed together. When they wither, the flower-heads turn brown and dry. Sometimes this happens only to the lower half of the bloom, while the upper part stays fresh and yellow.

HOP CLOVER   FLAX

HOUSE-LEEK

The leaflets grow in groups of three, and each is shaped like a pointed egg. Because of these groups of three, the plant has been given its other name of Hop Trefoil. "Trefoil" means "three leaves." Where the leaf-stalk joins the stem there are two green sheaths, put there as though to hide the join.

You can see the spreading masses of the Hop Clover all through the Summer.

FLAX

FROM one member of the Flax family we can make linen thread. The Pale Flax shown in the picture, however, is not useful in this way. It has a woody root, from which spring the smooth stems with their delicate branches.

The leaves are so narrow that they look like short blades of grass. They grow singly all the way up the stalks, first on one side, then on the other.

The flowers are pale-blue, veined with purple, and have five spreading petals. If you pluck them, the petals will fall very soon. They leave the tiny seed-vessels, which are neatly divided into sections, each holding a seed from which another Flax plant will grow.

You will find the Pale Flax growing in sandy fields and open spaces, as well as in waste places by the roadside. It blooms in June and July, but you may often see it again quite late in the Summer.

HOUSE-LEEK

You will have to look upwards if you want to see the House-leek. It likes to grow on the roof of an old cottage, or the top of an old wall. You would expect it to find it difficult to live there, but its thick, fleshy leaves store enough moisture to last for a long time. The leaves grow in pale-green rosettes, and have pink tips. They have stiff bristles all round the edges.

A long thick stem supports the flower, and this stem has more leaves, narrower than the others. The flowers are made up of twelve sharply-pointed pink petals. The bushy stamens are red, with golden heads.

The House-leek grows very easily. A piece from one plant will take root in almost any crack in a wall. At one time, country people liked to have it growing on their cottage roofs, because they believed that it protected them against lightning.

TANSY

This is a large bushy plant with feathery fern-like leaves. These have a bitter taste, and were once used in cakes and puddings! Because of the appearance of the leaves, another name for Tansy is Scented Fern.

TANSY

LESSER KNAPWEED   YELLOW TOAD-FLAX

The flowers are like so many golden buttons at the end of stalks branching out from the main stem. Each button is made up of many tube florets. The tubes stand on a round disc. Behind that is a double row of small, green, pointed leaves which make a cup.

The flower-heads are late in opening, so do not look for them before the end of July.

LESSER KNAPWEED

THIS is an Autumn flower, and has a purple flower-head set on a hard brown ball. It looks rather like a small thistle, without any prickles. In bud, the tube florets which make the flower-head are completely hidden inside the ball. After the flowers have withered, the balls still cling to the ends of the stalks.

The lower leaves have their edges cut into teeth. Those higher up are smooth, and smaller in size. All of them are dull-green, and rough to the touch. They have no stalks, and grow straight from the stem, which is tough and wiry.

YELLOW TOAD-FLAX

THIS plant likes dry places, and its blossoms can be seen as late as October. They make a bright-yellow spike at the top of a stiff stem. If you look at the open lips of the flower, you will see why the plant is called Toad-flax. You will think at once of the wide, drooping mouth of a toad.

There are many delicate blue-green leaves. They are long and pointed, and grow in pairs all the way up the stems.

The Toad-flax is a showy plant which spreads easily. It is sometimes called Wild Flax, or even Flax-weed.

BELL HEATHER

THIS is a bushy plant with tough wiry stems. In spite of its name you will probably think that its reddish-purple flower is shaped more like an egg than a bell. These flowers keep their colour a long time after being pulled. They grow in blunt clusters all round the stems and branches. The sepals are easily seen because they are green. The narrow, pointed leaves usually grow in threes, with some smaller leaflets among them. Because of their fineness, the plant has been given its other name of Fine-leaved Heath.

SILVERWEED

YOU will easily know the Silverweed because of its leaves. They are very deeply cut, and when they are half-open they seem almost white. Later they are dark-green above, while underneath they are covered with white silky hairs which give them a silvery look.

FINE-LEAVED HEATH OR BELL HEATHER

SILVERWEED

The flowers grow singly on long stalks. The five petals are yellow, and open out flat. The tip of a sepal can be seen between each petal.

The plant sends out long creepers which are often tinged with pink. These send down little roots which are the beginnings of new plants, and so the Silverweed never dies out.

An old-fashioned name for the Silverweed is Traveller's Ease. Because of its softness, the plant was used for soothing the tired feet of those who had been walking long distances. In days when most people had to do their travelling on foot, Silverweed must have been very popular!

IVY-LEAVED TOAD-FLAX

THE other name for this plant is Mother-of-thousands. Its thin, green stems spread very quickly over walls, throwing out tiny roots as they go. The leaves are divided into five. They are small and dark, like those of the Ivy. Underneath, they are often tinged with purple.

There are many flowers, and they are pale-lilac with yellow centres. The flower-head has a long spur or tube which holds the sweetness that the insects love. The seeds are held in a little ball.

The flowers bloom from May to September, and in some places at almost any time of the year. They give a yellow but not very lasting dye.

HAREBELL

In Scotland this is called the Bluebell. When you look at its blue, bell-like flowers, it is easy to see why. At its mouth, the bell is divided into five, and inside are the yellow heads of the five stamens. Behind the petals, the green sepals are divided into five sharp points like a star. The flower-stalks are long and slender, and the flowers grow sometimes singly, sometimes in clusters.

There are two kinds of leaves. Those on the main stem are narrow and pointed. Those coming from the root are nearly round, with edges cut into teeth.

The name Harebell may be explained by the fact that the plant likes to grow in the dry, hilly fields or open moors where the hare makes its home. Some people, however, prefer the spelling *Hair*bell, because they say the name then describes the delicate, slender stalks of the flowers.

VERVAIN

People once thought of this as a holy plant which could heal wounds.

It has stiff stems, and the branches which curve out from them are stiff too. The leaves can be of different shapes. The lower ones are deeply cut into, while the upper ones are narrower and more pointed. The flowers grow in long, slender spikes

IVY-LEAVED TOAD-FLAX

HAREBELL OR BLUEBELL OF SCOTLAND   VERVAIN

at the top of the stems and branches. They are
pale-lilac and very small. They are divided into
five sections. You will have to look very closely at
the wayside to see them at all, but if you are lucky
you will find them any time from July until
September.

Other names for the Vervain are Dove's Foot and
Pigeon's Foot. When people looked at the shape
of the leaves, they were reminded of these things.
Yet another name is Pigeon's Grass, because these
birds had a fondness for the places where the plant
was to be found.

LADY'S FINGERS
(Kidney Vetch)

THIS is another showy plant. It has strong pale-
green stems, thickly covered with soft hairs. The
narrow leaves also have this covering. They grow
in pairs up the stalk, with one big leaflet at the top.
They are deeply marked down the centre, and
often fold in two, showing that underneath they are
greyish-green.

You will know the Kidney Vetch because its
flower-heads, at the top of the stem, do not grow
singly, but in pairs. Each flower-head is made up
of many florets crowded together. They are
usually yellow, but can be red. The sepal-cup is
covered with fluffy down, and later on it swells up
to hold the seed-pod.

A frill of narrow pointed leaves, with no stalks,
stands out beneath each flower-head.

DO YOU KNOW THESE PLANTS?

1. Its name means "five leaves." Its flowers have five yellow petals.

2. It is a little like the plant just described, but its flowers have only four petals. Perhaps its name will make you think of something which people once thought it could cure!

3. This plant is the national emblem of Scotland.

4. Its deeply-cut leaves are green on top, and silvery underneath. The flowers grow singly, and have five yellow petals which open out flat.

5. This plant is very difficult to find. It has very small pale-lilac flowers, each divided into five sections. They grow in long, slender spikes.

6. The flower of this plant makes one think of the mouth of a toad. It likes dry places, and spreads very easily. The many leaves are long and pointed.

7. It has ferny leaves, and its yellow flowers are like buttons set on stalks.

8. This plant gives off a lovely perfume when crushed. Its flowers are small and purple, and its stems and leaves trail along the ground.

LADY'S FINGERS OR KIDNEY VETCH

Children's Book of Wild Flowers

PART IV.

List of Colour Plates

CREEPING BUTTERCUP

A NATURE NOTEBOOK

WHY not make your own book of the Wild Flowers which you know and have found for yourself? All you need is a notebook with a cover which will not come off easily.

In it you can write about the flowers you have seen on your walks. Give such details as where you found them, and at what time of year. The time of year is important, because perhaps the plant has come up specially early, and you may be seeing in February a flower which does not usually appear till much later. Leave a space for anything you can think of to explain why the plant should be there out of season. Perhaps the weather has been unusually mild; perhaps the plant is growing in a very sheltered spot, and so on.

Where the plant is found is important, because each district has its own group of flowers which are always found there, and any "strangers" should be specially noted. Try to account for them. The seeds may have been carried by a very high wind. Animals or birds may have brought them from a distance. You yourself may have helped, by carrying a seed such as that of the Traveller's Joy stuck to your coat.

If you find a plant you do not recognise, look at it very carefully. Note the appearance of the flower, the leaves, and their position on the stem. All these will help you to know the plant when you look it up later in your Wild Flower Book. If you are good at drawing, a sketch of the plant will be very useful.

No detail is too small to be left out of your notebook. Remember that you will want to refer to your notes perhaps a long time after writing them, when you will have forgotten most of the small but important details about how you found and identified a particular plant.

As time goes on, you will be able to compare your notes of one year with those of another. You will know whether the Spring flowers are early or late by comparison with those of the year before. Perhaps a plant which one year was growing in poor and stony soil has given up the struggle, and now cannot be found. Put this in your notebook too, and try to account for the plant's disappearance.

A special scrap-book can be kept for interesting Nature sketches and paragraphs from magazines and papers. You will be able to compare these notes with your own. Probably the writer will live in quite a different part of the country, and his observations will tell you how a plant found in your own district adapts itself to conditions in another.

SPOTTED ORCHIS   WATER FIGWORT

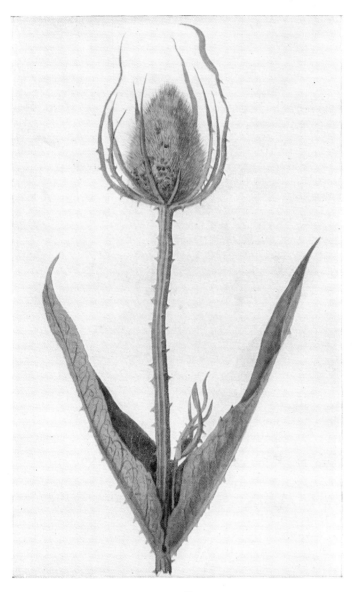

TEASEL

CREEPING BUTTERCUP

"Do you like butter?" You must often have played that game with buttercups. Did you know that there are several kinds of Buttercup? The one in the picture is the Creeping Buttercup. It spreads over the ground by means of long runners. Rootlets grow down from these, to steady the plant.

The flower has five glossy petals, and very often these open out flat like a saucer, in spite of being called Butter*cups*.

The leaves are divided into three, and their edges are deeply cut.

Farmers used to think that if their cows fed on Buttercups, the butter made from their milk would be specially rich and yellow in colour. The fact is, however, that cows find Buttercups too bitter in taste, and do not eat them at all!

SPOTTED ORCHIS

You will find this plant in Summer.

It grows on a solid stem, from roots which are divided like the fingers of a hand. The leaves taper to a point, and are splashed all over with dark purple. There are other Orchises with those markings, however, and it is more because of its flowers that this one in particular is called Spotted.

The flowers grow in a spike at the top of the stalk. Petals and sepals are both pale-lilac, spotted and streaked with purple. One broad petal, with wavy edges, is like a hanging lip, and behind it is a long tube. The other petals make a hood to cover the stamens. The flower is set at the top of what looks like a swollen stalk, but which is in fact the seed-vessel.

The flowers bloom unevenly. Those at the foot of the spike wither first. Above them are those fully out, and at the top are the buds.

WATER FIGWORT

This is a tall plant. The stem is very straight and stiff. It is square, and each corner grows out to what is almost a knife-edge.

Sometimes this plant is called Fiddle-strings, or Fiddles. Take two of the stems, and strip off the leaves. Then draw one stem across the other, and you will hear a decided squeak. It is not very like the sound of a fiddle, but it is the reason for this name being given to the Water Figwort.

The leaves are long and heart-shaped, and grow in pairs. Have you ever rubbed them between your hands? They make a slight soapy lather, and sometimes the plant is called Soapleaves because of this.

The flowers are very small. They grow in loose clusters at the ends of the stem and branches. In bud they are brown, and when open they are reddish-purple. They are round, with five divisions. Four of these are upright, and one is turned downwards. In the centre are the bright-yellow heads of the stamens.

GERMANDER SPEEDWELL OR BIRD'S-EYE

FIELD SCABIOUS

TEASEL

THIS is a tall, pale-green plant, easily seen. It has a thick, strong stem, covered with sharp prickles. The leaves have no stalks, and grow from the stem in pairs. Where they clasp the stem, they make a little cup, which is often filled with rain or dew. The leaves are prickly underneath, so be careful when you touch them.

The flowers grow in a prickly head at the top of the plant. Tiny purple florets are pressed together between green prickles. Long narrow leaflets curve upwards round the flower-head, and these too are prickly.

One of the Teasels, called the Fuller's Teasel, is used by cloth-makers. The cloth is brushed with the flower-heads, and their little hooks catch in the material and give it a fluffy surface.

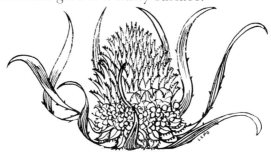

FIELD SCABIOUS

THIS is a bristly plant. The stem and leaves are covered with hairs. The leaves are divided into long, narrow fingers on each side of a central stalk.

The flower-head has a long, stiff stalk of its own. Many florets crowd together to look like a single flower. Those in the centre are reddish-pink tubes. Round them is a border of lilac-blue ones. These have straps which grow out like a frill round the flower-head.

There are many stamens sticking out like pins all over the flower-head. These have given the plant its other name of Lady's Pincushion. You can find these pincushions in July and August.

GERMANDER SPEEDWELL

LONG ago, "Speed well" was another way of saying "Goodbye." Perhaps this plant got its name because its petals fall almost as soon as the flower is plucked.

You will easily see the bright blue of the Speedwell, where it grows in the banks and woods. The flower is divided into four sections, making a shallow cup. In the centre is a small white circle, like an eye. Sometimes the flower is called Bird's Eye. Two stamens with crimson heads come from the white "eye." There are four narrow green sepals.

The oval leaves are dark-green and hairy, with edges cut into little teeth. The slender flower-stems rise from between leaf and main stem.

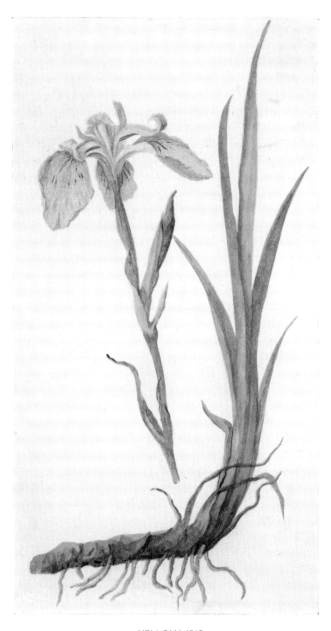

YELLOW IRIS

COMFREY

YELLOW IRIS

BE careful not to get wet when you look for this plant. It is always found near water.

The leaves are long and pointed, and their edges are sharp, like swords.

There is no mistaking the flowers of the Iris. In bud they are covered by a green sheath. When they open, the petals and sepals are almost the same colour. The large parts of the flower are the sepals. They are yellow, streaked with deeper orange. They fold back from a short yellow tube, and hang down like flags—another name for the Iris is the Water Flag. Between each sepal is a small, paler-yellow petal. From the centre of the flower come what look like three more petals, but they are really part of the column which rises from the seed-vessel.

In Autumn the seed-vessel becomes very large and then bursts into three parts, with rows of dark-brown seeds neatly packed inside.

COMFREY

THIS is a moisture-loving plant. It was once thought to be a cure for bruises.

It grows in large, leafy clumps. The stem is hollow, and ridged up and down. Both it and the narrow, pointed leaves are covered with hairs. The leaves which grow from the root can be very big.

16

The flowers may be of different colours. Often they are purple, while the buds are pink. The short flower-stalks curl round on themselves while the flower is still in bud. When it opens, they uncurl, and the flowers hang in drooping clusters. They are like little bells, so much so that in some parts of the country they are called Church-bells. Each flower has five petals. The long thread from the seed-vessel sticks out like a needle, and is there long after the flower has fallen.

MEADOWSWEET

LONG ago, when people had no carpets for their floors, they used to scatter sweet-scented flowers and herbs instead. We are told that Queen Elizabeth liked to have her rooms strewn with Meadowsweet. The flowers of the Queen of the Meadow, as the plant is sometimes called, have a special fragrance, and this is what attracts insects to them. They are creamy-white, with five small petals and a bush of yellow stamens. There are five green sepals which fold back against the stem when the petals have withered. The flowers cluster at the ends of the stem and its branches. They are so delicate that they give the plant a lacy appearance.

The leaves are deeply wrinkled. They are green above and greyer underneath. Two large leaves grow turn about with two small ones. At the end of each leaf-stalk is a leaflet divided into three.

The stem is slender and stained with red.

MEADOWSWEET

EARLY PURPLE ORCHIS

EARLY PURPLE ORCHIS

As its name tells you, this plant blooms in early
Spring. The flowers are strangely shaped, and it
is difficult to tell petals and sepals apart, as they
are all purple. One petal hangs down like a lip,
and this one has a long tube at the back. Two
others stand straight up to form a hood. The
flower is shaped in the same way as the Spotted
Orchis, which has been described earlier. Here
and there are patches of darker and lighter purple.

The seed-vessel looks like a twisted purple stalk.
Where it joins the flower-stem there is always a
narrow purple leaf. The flower-stem is thick and
juicy.

The leaves have no stalks, and grow in a cluster
close to the ground. They are long and broad,
and covered with dark-purple spots.

The root looks like two knobs. From these the
plant gets its food. Many white rootlets grow out
from them.

WILD CARROT

This is an umbrella plant, with masses of tiny white
flowers at the end of green spokes. Many plants
have flower-heads like this, but the Wild Carrot
can easily be recognised. Before the flowers are
fully out, their spokes stand straight up. The buds
are often tinged with pink, but the open florets

are usually white. The very centre of the flower-head sometimes remains pink. After the florets have withered, the spokes curve inwards, and what was the flower-head now looks more like a bird's nest!

The leaves of the Wild Carrot are feathery, like ferns. Their stalks come from sheaths which hold the stem.

The stem itself helps you to know the Wild Carrot. Most umbrella plants have hollow stems, but this one is solid.

FORGET-ME-NOT

THERE are many kinds of Forget-me-not, but the loveliest is the one which likes marshy places. It is a tall, straggling plant, with bright-green leaves clasping the stem. They are shiny, as though newly dipped in water, and have smooth edges.

The flower-stalks are long and grow on alternate sides of the stem. The flowers are pink in bud. Those nearest the foot of the stalk come out first, and do not last very long. The fully-opened flowers are just above them, and the buds are at the top.

The five petals of the opened flower are blue, and lie like a wheel. In the centre is a bright-yellow eye. The stamens are hidden in a small blue tube below the petals.

WILD CARROT

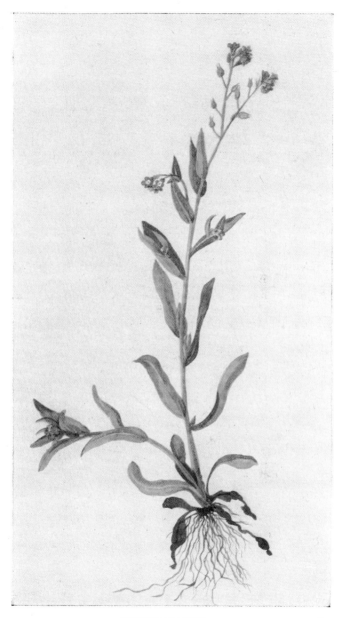

FORGET-ME-NOT

GREAT WILLOW HERB

THERE are several kinds of Willow Herb. The one in the picture likes to grow near water. It is a tall plant, covered with soft hairs. The leaves grow from the stem, which they clasp in the same way as those of the Teasel. They are long and narrow, with uneven edges.

The flowers grow in showy clusters. They are usually rose-pink, with four petals, notched at the edges. These are set in a green, hairy sepal-cup.

The flowers have what look like long reddish stalks, but after the petals have fallen these split into four strips which curl back on themselves. The "stalk" can now be seen to be holding the seeds of the new plants. Each seed has a parachute of white hairs to help it to float away from the parent plant.

HAIRY MINT

THIS is a plant which likes damp places, and because of this it is often called Water Mint. It spreads easily and is often seen in large masses. The stems are square, and covered with hairs. The leaves are also hairy. They grow in pairs, and are oval, with uneven edges.

The flowers grow closely together at the top of the main stem, or lower down where the leaf-stalks spring. Each lilac-coloured flower-head is made up of many tiny tubes. Four stamens with crimson heads stick out from the mouth of each tube. Just below the flower-head, there is often a pair of small oval leaves.

The Hairy Mint has the strong scent of the Garden Mint, but it is not good to eat.

CORNFLOWER

THE brilliant blue of the Cornflower is a familiar sight in the ripening fields. It is related to the Thistle, though of course it has no prickles. The flower-head is made up of many florets. Those on the outside are blue tubes, opening out into trumpets. The florets in the centre are much smaller, and their blue is tinged with pink.

The flower-heads come from a cup of green scales pressed very closely together.

The stem and leaves are often covered with white woolly down. The stem is very tough, and used to blunt the farmers' sickles in the days when they cut corn with these tools. Most of the leaves are long and narrow, like grass. The lower ones sometimes have their edges cut into teeth.

The Cornflower has many other names, mostly connected with its colour. By some it is called Blue-bonnets, and by others, Blue-buttons.

One strange name is Break-your-spectacles. There is no obvious reason for this. Perhaps people thought that if they plucked a cornflower they would be likely to break their spectacles very soon afterwards. Parsley is another plant which was once supposed to have an unlucky effect on spectacles!

GREAT WILLOW HERB

CORNFLOWER   HAIRY MINT

SUNDEW

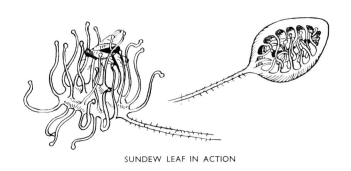

SUNDEW LEAF IN ACTION

THE Sundew flowers are white, with five petals, and they grow on a long stem. They will not help you to recognise the plant, however, for they open only in very strong sunshine, and not always then. What you are most likely to see is a row of green buds.

The leaves are what make the Sundew different from other plants. They grow out in a rosette at the end of long, reddish stalks which lie along the ground. They are spoon-shaped, and covered with short, reddish hairs. At the tip of each hair is a tiny drop of what looks like dew. Touch it, and you will find it sticky. This is what attracts insects. They are then caught in the stickiness, and cannot fly away. Their struggles irritate the whole leaf. The hairs bend over, and the leaf curls inwards to make a prison. In this way the Sundew gets its food. This sounds very cruel, but the ground in which it grows is so poor, that the plant is forced to look for nourishment elsewhere.

BOG ASPHODEL

THIS is a wiry plant, with a stiff stem. So stiff is it, that another name for Bog Asphodel is King's Spear. The leaves are like rough blades of grass, and have no stalks. They are mostly at the foot of the stem. On the stem itself are other small leaves, pressing against it like scales.

The flowers grow in a spike near the top of the stem. They are orange-yellow, with petals and sepals of the same colour. These open to make a six-pointed star. When the seeds are ripening, the star closes and becomes a cup. The six stamens in the centre of the flower are yellow and woolly, with red tops.

The plants of the Bog Asphodel like to grow together, in a clump.

MARSH MARIGOLD

PERHAPS you call this plant the Kingcup. It belongs to the same family as the Buttercup. It is one of the showiest flowers of Spring. It has no petals, but the five sepals are bright-yellow and glossy. In the midst of them is a big bunch of yellow stamens.

The leaves are also big and glossy. They have crinkled edges, and are covered with a network of veins.

SUNDEW   BOG ASPHODEL

MARSH MARIGOLD   COWSLIP

The flower-stalks are hollow, and easily broken. When you pull the flowers, the stalks soon become soft. To make them stiff again, you must put them in water. This plant likes plenty of water.

In some parts of the country, Marsh Marigolds are called May-bubbles. You will understand why, if you look at the flowers when they are partly closed. They are like big, golden bubbles.

COWSLIP

THE Cowslip will probably make you think of the Primrose. The leaves of both are dark-green and crinkled, but those of the Cowslip are more pointed and more deeply veined towards the centre.

The main difference lies in the flowers. The Cowslip has several flowers drooping from each stalk, while the Primrose flowers grow singly. Each flower has a yellow tube set in a green sepal-cup. Round the mouth of the tube are five small yellow petals, each with a reddish-orange spot at the foot. Cowslip flowers contain a large quantity of honey.

The Cowslip is like the Primrose again in that it can be Pin-eyed or Thrum-eyed. Do you remember what that meant?

You will see Cowslips in flower in Spring or early Summer.

COMMON FLEABANE

THIS whole plant has a woolly appearance. The round stem is covered with down, and so are the many leaves. These grow very thickly, and have wavy edges. They are heart-shaped.

The flowers look like big yellow daisies. They grow at the ends of branches which stand out like arms near the top of the main stem. Each flower-head is made up of dozens of ray and tube florets. The tubes in the centre are a darker yellow than the ray florets which encircle them.

Another name for this plant is Harvest Flower, because it is at its best at that time of year. It has yet another name, Herb Christopher, after St Christopher who (as an old story says) carried Christ across a river. Where Christ told him to set his staff in the ground, flowers sprang up, and the story tells that this is the one which St Christopher gathered.

COMMON FLEABANE